MIMESIS
INTERNATIONAL

LITERATURE

n. 11

Farian Sabahi

WE WOMEN OF TEHRAN

MIMESIS
INTERNATIONAL

First published in 2013 (i Corsivi, Corriere della Sera) and in 2014 (Mimesis Edizioni, Milan). Also available in French (Éditions Mimésis)

Translated by Catherine Bolton

Isbn: 9788869773266
Book series: *Literature*, n. 11

SUMMARY

To my son Atesh, dozd-e delam

I have always landed in Tehran at night. A sea of lights is visible from the airplane window: the houses have no blinds or shutters and there's a faint glimmer coming from every apartment.

Nowhere in the world do entire families go out to welcome relatives returning from distant lands. But it happens in Tehran, so there are huge crowds at the airport. Everybody all together, with their inevitable bouquets. Parents, grandparents, brothers and sisters, aunts and uncles, grandchildren, nieces and nephews. Old people and children. Family members are the ones who grab your cart stacked high with luggage. Porters? They don't even attempt to approach you! A bit like the Italians when emigrants returned. A faded postcard.

Ever since I was little the image of the new day being born has been etched on my mind. I'm in a cab and we go through Azadì Square: in Persian *azadì* means freedom. And I'm always astonished by that tower of white marble, marble from the region of Isfahan. It stands out against the sky –

which changes colour at that very moment – as the capital slowly wakes up.

* * *

Khosh amadid, welcome to Tehran! These pages are dedicated to those of you who, despite the winds of war, have decided to venture to Iran. "Life is but a journey, to travel is to live twice", wrote Omar Khayyam. The art of living and the art of travelling mirror each other. Travelling is a way to discover ourselves, because as long as you remain inside your shop or home, you will not truly be a person: get out and roam the world, before the day you ultimately leave it.

Before embarking on a journey, Persians always hold a small ceremony. On a tray, they place the Quran and two objects: a bowl of water with flower petals, as the transparency shows the purity of the heart and the vision that God has of man's journey toward him, and then a dish of wheat, the sign of prosperity and success. Someone holds up the tray with both hands and the traveller walks under it three times, and each time he kisses the Quran. Then he looks at his image in the mirror, the symbol of the light of fate. Crossing the threshold, the traveller walks away and water is sprinkled on the ground where he stepped.

Did you forget something when you left? It doesn't matter: it's a sign that you'll return.

* * *

Tehran is the capital of Iran, a country that is five and a half times the size of Italy. It is crisscrossed by countless caravan routes: the silk road, the spice road, the road of gems. These roads were travelled by merchants, intellectuals, artists, men of faith. Three thousand years of history have refined the soul of this population. A noble soul, proud of its identity because, as Nezamì wrote, "The world is a body, Iran its heart." It is a soul that finds a second mother tongue in poetry.

We are an Indo-European people, like you. We are not Arabs, as people sometimes think. Persia was the name of our country until the 1930s, the name given to it by the English, after Fars, the central region. Reza Shah decided to distance himself from British imperialism and in 1936 he chose the name *Iran*: *Persia* referred only to the province of Fars and was associated with the decadence of the Qajar dynasty, whereas *Iran* evokes the glory of the ancient Persian Empire.

For Herodotus, the Persians were the people most open to foreign customs. Conquered by Alexander the Great and then the Arabs, sacked by the Mongols and by Tamerlane, under Russian and English protection but never a colony, Iran has always maintained its culture, although it was open to foreign influences, both ancient and modern. The Magi were Persians. They went to visit Jesus, bearing gold, frankincense and myrrh. They were the priests of Zoroaster, the prophet who spread monotheism from the Iranian Plateau.

Iran: a multiethnic, multicultural and multireligious land, playing a leading role in the Muslim civilization – Arab and non-Arab alike – and making its influence felt well beyond its current borders. What is now defined as the *Iranian world* is a cultural space. It extends from east of Iran to northern India, going through Central Asia. It is a world that is hard to grasp and, in certain ways, it is paradoxical. It is a country with terrible press, above all after the 1979 revolution but even more so today. But these are only rumours. Just noise. Because, as a Middle Eastern proverb says, "the dogs bark but the caravan moves on".

* * *

Tehran, a faraway city, although not that much. It is on the 35th parallel north, like the Italian island of Lampedusa. There are singular affinities between Tehran and southern Italy. In Tehran, as in Italy, people address each other with the formal rather than the informal "you": we use the word *shomà* to address people we don't know and those to whom we show respect, such as when we talk to the elderly, grandparents included. Just like they do in southern Italy.

Family encounters are crowded and noisy. If they have guests, Persians offer a wealth of food and drinks. A piece of advice: never empty your cup, or they will fill it up again. If you don't eat, your host will be offended, just as in southern Italy, where for centuries women were in a subordinate position, veiled in black. They did not sit at the table with men. And in the street they would walk a step behind them.

In Iran there are Ashura processions to commemorate the death of Imam Hossein, Muhammad's grandson, who was killed in 680 CE on the plain of Kerbela. Dressed in mourning clothes, the men walk through the city streets, weeping and cursing Hossein's murderers. To the rhythm of drums and cymbals, they pound their chests and some strike their heads. They are careful not to shed any blood, however, because after the 1979 Revolution the ayatollahs outlawed this: Islam forbids hurting oneself.

In southern Italy there are processions with flagellants. Even today in the Calabrian town of Nocera Terinese, during the celebrations for Holy Saturday some of the faithful – the so-called *vattienti* – strike their legs with a sharp instrument. And in Guardia Sanframondi, in the province of Benevento, the week after the 15th of August people celebrate the septennial rituals in honour of Our Lady of the Assumption: on Sunday, wearing a white habit with a hood and their chests partly bared, the penitents scourge themselves, just as was done in the Middle Ages. In their right hand they hold a wooden cross, in their left a cork cilice covered with thorns or a sponge full of needles and soaked in wine. Then they strike their chests until they bleed.

These are singular affinities, perhaps the legacy of southern Italy's Islamic and Shiite past. As in southern Italy, in Tehran too honour leads to interminable and absurd escalations, to cock fights. Look at those two cars: they go into a street where only one car can pass, and they both continue until they are face to face. Then the drivers start to argue, first leaning from the window and then getting out of their cars.

* * *

Tehran is in the north, at the foot of the Elburz Mountains, at an altitude ranging from 1,200 to 1,700 metres. In spring, the sky is barren and blue. In winter the mountains are covered with ice and bluish snow glistening in the sun and blinding you. The ice drinks in the sunshine. According to the Avesta, the book sacred to the Zoroastrians, High Hara is the first mountain in the world, a source of light and water. Its roots burrow deep into the soil, whereas its peak took 800 years to rise and it is now anchored to the sky.

Tehran is a divided city: mountains to the north, desert to the south. The northern slopes are home to the wealthy, who snub the Islamic Republic, and their women – their noses redone and wearing heavy makeup – cover only part of their hair with a scarf. They wear the chador only to go to the Masumeh Shrine in the holy city of Qum.

To the south is the bazaar: heaps of spices, samovars for tea, colourful wool carpets. The tiny shops conceal incredible treasures. In 1858 Arthur de Gobineau wrote that "all Persians are brokers. Everyone sells or pawns what they own. And when I say everyone, I mean everyone: the king pawns his jewels, his wives their trinkets; the scholar gets loans against his books and the landowner against his fields. There is no man or woman without debts, and perhaps there is no

15

person so indebted that, in turn, he doesn't have his own debtors. Around holiday time, half of the city lends money to the other half."[1] Even today, the Persians love to bargain at the bazaar. They spin everything out and waste time in pleasantries. It is there, in those southern quarters, that the *faghir* live: the poor, as they are called in Persian. They are grateful towards the authorities and the women wear the chador.

Tehran is a divided city: divided by two large thoroughfares. The first is Vali Asr, dedicated to the symbol of the Shia. Mehdi the Vali Asr, the Lord of the Twilight. It is a tree-lined street that, flanking the city's most important torrent, linked historic Tehran with the summer residences of nobles and merchants in the lush greenery of the villages of Niavaran, Kakh Qajar, Shemiran and Tajrish, and the one that would later become Farmanieh, going through the prevalently Christian village of Vanak. When the torrent was channelled, Vali Asr became a six-lane boulevard stretching for over twenty kilometres, lined with ancient plane-trees and rivulets of running water. It connects the ancient palaces of Sad 'Abad (to the north) with the railway station south of the bazaar, skirting Park-e Mellat and hundreds of

---

1   Arthur Gobineau, *Trois ans en Asie*, Paris: Librairie de L. Hachette et C[ie] 1858, p. 254.

shops small and large, shopping centres, popular *chelo kabab* and fashionable restaurants, banks and the headquarters of important companies. The other main road is Enghelab Avenue, Islamic Revolution Street, where the University of Tehran is located: it runs from east to west to the Azadì Tower. Vali Asr and Enghelab Avenue are the new names that, in 1979, the revolutionaries gave to streets dating to the monarchy, when they were called Pahlavi Avenue (and, for a very short time, Mossadegh Boulevard) and Reza Shah Avenue.

* * *

It takes weeks to get accustomed to Tehran's climate. A dry throat, the need to blow your nose constantly and shortness of breath are problems triggered by the city's altitude.

As in Italy, July is the hottest month and January the coldest. In winter it snows in the higher districts, while in the lower-class ones to the south the snow melts immediately. In the summer the heat is dry; your clothes don't stick to your skin even when it's forty degrees outside. The sun shines all the time, every morning. It's a given for us. Sometimes a strange wind blows. It comes from the west, from Iraq. From the desert. It brings sand with it: red sand. Though it is rare, every so often it happens. It feels like being in the middle of a sandstorm, on another planet.

Tehran: a formless city of twelve million inhabitants – without counting the suburbs. Fifty kilometres in diameter. Millions of vehicles on the road. The air is unbreathable. Tehran has donned the Western uniform of smog. In more than one way, it resembles a Western outpost. It is a political, administrative, economic and cultural centre. For one reason or another, everyone comes through Tehran. Today the hotels are packed with people who think they can do business here. Russians and Chinese are ready to replace the Europeans, forced to leave because of sanctions.

Tehran is not a pretty city. There is no comparison with Isfahan, the ancient capital referred to as *nesf-e jahan*, half of the world, because it holds thousands of architectural wonders. Along with Cairo and Istanbul, Tehran is one of the three megalopolises of the Middle East. But in comparison, Tehran is a strange city. Cairo was built on the banks of the Nile and Istanbul on the Bosporus. Tehran is at the foot of a mountain chain rising to an altitude of 4,000 metres on a semi-desert plateau. It has no real river, nor any access to the sea.

Moreover, it is not an ancient city. Tehran has been the capital since the eighteenth century.

The first emperor of the Qajar dynasty worried about the Russians, who were threatening the northern boundary, and the Turkomans, Uzbeks and Kyrgyz, who put pressure on the country and raided it from the north-east. And from the north-east there came invasions by the Mongols, a brutal population. In *Il Milione* – known in English as *The Travels of Marco Polo* – the Venetian tells the story of Nayan, whose uncle rolled him up in a carpet so tightly that he suffocated: he did not want to shed the blood of a descendant of Genghis Khan on the earth. The same fate awaited the last caliph Al-Musta'sim, defeated by the Mongol army led by Hülegü: after the fall of Baghdad in 1258, the Mongols had the caliph rolled up in a carpet and then crushed by horses.

* * *

The crossroads of East and West, protected by mountains to the north and situated along the caravan roads leading to the oases of the central and southern areas, Tehran was in a strategic position to control the empire. But this was not enough to save it from invasion: one of the Qajar emperors tried to keep Russian appetites in check, but in 1828 Russia managed to wrest Armenia, Georgia and Azerbaijan from him. And in the meantime, the English were arriving from the south. They were willing to do anything to gain control over the road to the Indies, to their colonies.

Since then, in Tehran we have had little tolerance for foreign interference. This sentiment grew after 1951, when Prime Minister Mossadegh had the temerity to nationalize oil, which had been exploited until then by the West. The prime minister ended up featured on the cover of *TIME*. But the English and Americans decided that they would make him pay for it. And in 1953 Mossadegh fell victim to a coup d'état.

* * *

Tehran is not a pretty city. Here and there you see buildings that are only half finished. Forgotten. Abandoned to their fate. Maybe money ran out. They look like skeletons in the middle of buildings that resemble anthills. So many skyscrapers, rising like mushrooms. They bought entire quarters, demolished two- and three-storey houses, and built huge skyscrapers. And made money hand over fist. The town plan? There is one, but, as an old Middle Eastern proverb says, "the smell of money can divert rivers".

Tehran is not a pretty city, and like a woman who knows she isn't pretty, she makes the most of her seductive charms. Tehran is the heart of Iran, its capital. This is where policies are decided. This is where the economy unfolds. This is where intellectuals live, the ones who count: writers, directors, artists. Those you probably know too, those who have been translated. They have won the Golden Bear in Berlin and the Golden Palm in Cannes. Tough people, people who don't run away, people who don't go to live somewhere else.

Tehran has two symbols: the Azadì Tower and the Milad Tower. Rising to a height of 435 metres, the top is a twelve-storey structure. Situated between Shahrak-e Gharb and the Gisha district, the Milad Tower is a concrete structure. It looks like a modern building, but its base is octagonal, a tribute to traditional Persian architecture. Commenced in 2000, it was completed seven years later. It is reminiscent of the BT Tower, the telecommunications tower in London, and the Milad Tower likewise has a space for the state television and radio broadcast company. At the speed of seven meters per second, six lifts go up to a conference centre, the lobby of a five-star hotel and a restaurant with a view of the city that is a bit too expensive for the average person.

Imposing and bizarre, made of white marble, it does not go unnoticed: it is the Azadì Tower – the Freedom Tower – that we have already mentioned. It was built in 1971 by a *bahai* architect, Hossein Amanat. He was exiled after the revolution because in the Seventies the *bahais* had been too close to the shah and because Islam does not contemplate other prophets after Muhammad, so their religion – monotheistic – is heresy. Today the Freedom Tower is a cultural complex. Inside there is a museum with a copy of the Cyrus Cylinder, commissioned by the sovereign who promised the Jewish people they could return to Jerusalem and rebuild the Temple, giving them the money to do so. The original of the Cyrus Cylinder is at the British Museum. It was discovered in 1879 by the Assyro-British archaeologist Hormuz Rassam during the excavation of the Babylonian Temple of Marduk in what is now Iraq. The expedition had been funded by the British Museum, which is why the museum kept the cylinder.

The Cyrus Cylinder is the first universal declaration of human rights, on a par with the Magna Carta and the American Constitution: as far as we know, the Cyrus Cylinder was the first attempt to administrata a society, a state, with people of different nationalities and faiths. It is a hymn to liberty, to the right to imagine how society could – and should – be, both then and now. It is a text from nearly 2,600 years ago, but it is current even today for the many cities on the planet in which people of different nationalities and religions live together.

White is the colour of the Azadì Tower. Turquoise is our stone. It is porous and deteriorates in contact with soap and perfume. Pliny wrote that it is attacked by oils and balsams; it is one of the most delicate stones and incorrect treatment can change its colour. In *Il Milione*, Marco Polo wrote that in the kingdom of Kerman, which had just been conquered by the Tatars, there are many stones known as *turquoise*. This is what the Europeans call it, perhaps because initially the Turks were the ones who sold it, but its name in Persian is different: *firuzeh*. In Persian *firouz* means "champion", but *firuzeh* is simply the name of a stone. It is widely appreciated in Persia, although it is thought that turquoises are the bones of people who died for love: it is best to avoid wearing them, because they make love unhappy.

On 1 February 1979 millions of people gathered in Azadì Square. They were celebrating the return of the Ayatollah Khomeini after fourteen years in exile. This was the beginning of the Islamic Revolution. The shah had fled two weeks earlier. He had been in power since 1941 and Europe's glossy magazines often wrote about him, that he had been married three times. But not to Maria Gabriella of Savoy, despite discussions and negotiations between the two families, between members of the two governments, and even between the Vatican and the ulemas in the holy city of Qum. It was they – the Catholic and Shiite religious authorities – who had been unable to reach an agreement.

His first wife was Fawzia, sister of the Egyptian king Faruq. The wedding was orchestrated in 1939 by Mohammad Reza's father, the founder of the Pahlavi dynasty. He had become emperor, but he was only an army man with a humble background, and with that marriage he would fully enter the club of the Middle Eastern monarchies. Fawzia looked like a beautiful Hollywood actress. On 21 September 1942 she appeared on the cover of *Life* in an artist's portrait. Cecil Beaton described her as an "Asian Venus" with "a perfect heart-shaped face and strangely pale but piercing blue eyes".

These ingredients were not enough to make the marriage last, also because the couple had just one daughter, Shahnaz, but the monarchy needed a male heir. Fawzia returned to Cairo and, after the Egyptian revolution of 1952, she went to live in Switzerland. She died on 2 July 2013, in Alexandria, at the age of 91.

The shah's second wife was Soraya Esfandiary Bakhtiari, who had an Iranian father and a German mother, a Jew of Russian extraction. Young and beautiful, Soraya resembled Ava Gardner. With her brother, she was the heir to the powerful tribal confederation of the Bakhtiari. Their lands, expropriated by the shah, held the country's most important oilfields. Although it was an arranged marriage, it was also one of great passion: in this case, the one did not exclude the other. They were married in 1951, but the shah divorced her in 1958 because she was unable to bear him children. She went to live in France and decided to become an actress. Soraya fell in love with the Italian director Franco Indovina, who would later die tragically in a plane crash at Punta Raisi, near Palermo. Rumours circulated about a conspiracy. She – a.k.a. the Sad Princess – died in Paris in 2001, at the age of 69.

In 1959 the shah married Farah Diba, the daughter of a captain who had graduated from the French Military Academy of St. Cyr, as befitting certain aristocrats. Her grandfather had been a diplomat, serving as an ambassador in Russia at the Romanov court. Farah Diba attended the Italian kindergarten in Tehran, then went to the French school, and finally moved to Paris to study architecture. The government granted scholarships and the shah met with students abroad, where he saw the young Farah at the Iranian embassy in Paris. They would go on to have four children, two boys and two girls. The eldest, Reza, is now 53, lives in Potomac, Maryland, and is an American citizen. His brother Ali-Reza committed suicide in 2011, just as his sister Leila had done ten years earlier. And then there is Farahnaz. She is 50 and lives in New York.[2] She was 4 when her father was crowned emperor. For the occasion, in her dark hair, the girl wore a diamond tiara specially made for her by Van Cleef & Arpels.

* * *

Tehran is a new city but no one knows what its name means. It may mean "those who hunt or shoot", but it could mean "hot place". These are suppositions. It is impossible to find the meaning of the name of a city without memory. It has no memory of the great Persian emperors, nor of Darius, who lost the war against Alexander the Great.

During the Mongol era the ravines north of Rey were referred to as Teherun, but it was a location close to modern-day Tehran that was once famous. It was called Rey, the biblical Rhages. It

2   Reza Pahlavi II was born 31 October 1960; Fahranaz was born 12 March 1963.

26

is said that this was the birthplace of the prophet Zoroaster, who taught the Persians three rules of life: good thoughts, good words, good actions. Zoroaster: for him, fire – *atash* – was the vital principle. The dispenser of strength, power, knowledge and the creator of all things. Fire: the symbol of knowledge and revelation.

Today, that city is still called Shahr-e Rey. The mausoleum of Bibi Shahr Banu still stands there. It is a sanctuary for women alone, to commemorate the daughter of the last Sassanid emperor, Yazdagerd III: captured by the Arabs and taken to Medina, she was married off to Hossein, son of the Imam Ali. She bore him a son, Ali Zayn-al-Abedin, who would become the fourth Shiite Imam. After the Battle of Kerbela and her husband's death, Bibi Shahr Banu escaped to Persia, pursued by his enemies. About to be captured near Rey, she desperately invoked God. But instead of crying *Yallahu*, she was only able to sigh *Ya kuh*: "O mountain!" And the mountain miraculously opened up. Bibi Shahr Banu lived amid those rocks and a temple was built there. A Persian with a Jewish mother (her paternal grandfather was the great rabbi of the Sassanid Empire), she was the mother of the survivor of the massacre at Kerbela, the man who would become the fourth Imam.

A nearby mountain would be named after her, after Bibi Shahr Banu. Who knows? Perhaps it's true or maybe it's legend. It is a matter of faith. According to some, Bibi Shahr Banu was not the wife of Imam Hossein. The Persians supposedly invented her. That sanctuary was dedicated to the goddess of fertility and water, Anahita, a goddess of the pre-Islamic tradition, and a deity well before the Achaemenids: a young woman with a taut and slender body, driving a chariot drawn by four horses: wind, rain, cloud and sleet. In mythology, she is the one who purifies the male seed and the woman's womb, who ensures the purity of a mother's milk. She was considered the symbol of life and warriors carried her into battle to ensure their safe return and victory. They prayed to her and offered sacrifices. After converting to Islam, Persians hid the truth, thus saving the temple of Anahita, the goddess who has nothing to do with Islam.

* * *

Most of us are Muslim, but in our own way. We belong to the Shiite minority, the Shia, the faction of Imam Ali. Faithful to Muhammad and an able warrior of great moral stature, fair in administering war booty and magnanimous towards prisoners, he was the Prophet's cousin and married the latter's favourite daughter Fatimah, the only one of his children to survive. She gave birth to Hassan and Hossein.

According to the Shiites, a few months before Muhammad's death Ali was officially invested to succeed him in the site of Ghadir Khumm, halfway between Mecca and Medina. The Prophet stopped there with his followers after making his last pilgrimage to Mecca. Here Muhammad took Ali by the hand, declaring that anyone who recognized him as the protector-lord of the faithful would have Ali as his protector-lord. It is an episode that the Sunni do not refute, but they downplay it, considering it merely a sign of esteem and affection.

When the Prophet died in 632, the faithful had to decide who would head the community. A considerable number of Muslims thought that leadership should go to a vicar, a *khalifa*, to be elected among a group of sages who could decide following established tribal mechanisms. These notables were favourable towards Abu Bakr, Muhammad's Companion, father of his young and favourite wife Aisha and thus the Prophet's father-in-law. Abu Bakr became caliph, and would be succeeded by Omar and Uthman, also the Prophet's Companions. Ali considered them usurpers, but kept his distance without fomenting dissent, until one day during Uthman's caliphate he was bold enough to take a stand. The fourth caliph, Ali would be opposed by the governor of Syria, Mu'awiya, and Aisha, with whom there was no love lost. Life was not easy for Ali, but with him there arose the principle of the legitimate succession of Muhammad's descendants through his daughter Fatimah, progeny vested with religious and temporal power.

The Shia has been Iran's state religion since 1501, a political decision made by Shah Ismail, a ruler from the Safavid dynasty: to have us convert to make us *different* from the Ottoman enemy – Sunni – threatening our borders. The rivalry between Sunni and Shiites is fierce, to the point that, as Jane Dieulafoy wrote in 1885, "they do not seem to belong to the same religion. Everything divides them, even colours: the former say that Muhammad's turban was blue, the latter swear it was the colour of grass."

The Shia is now part of our identity. But we are not all Muslims. Iran is a mosaic of people, ethnic groups, languages and religions. Iran is a country that, as the English traveller Freya Stark observed, is a refuge for any anti-governmental heresy. We are also rather superstitious, despite our religious convictions: just like the Italians. In

Persia, when someone sneezes we say *sabr amad*, "patience came". This patience must be exercised and, in fact, before leaving you wait a few minutes to avoid bad luck. We fear the evil eye, which in Persian we call *cheshm zadan*. That is why we hate it when someone points to our child in the cradle and says *What a beautiful baby!* It could bring us bad luck.

And we also believe in *jinn*, genies: creatures that are part human and part fantastical, and with supernatural powers. They are often mentioned in the Quran, where an entire chapter is devoted to them. The *jinn* abound in literature. There are those who help human beings and even the Imams, while others thwart us in every way; some know how to fly, with or without wings; others can appear in the form of animals – dogs and donkeys – and some can even acquire human features, like the genie in Aladdin's lamp!

We respect the religions of the book. Christians, Jews and Zoroastrians cannot proselytize. But they have freedom of worship. And for over a hundred years they have elected their deputies. In Tehran there are churches and synagogues, because respect for other faiths has an ancient history. And perhaps we learned dissimulation from the Jews, from their queen, Esther. Her tomb is in Iran: at Hamedan, ancient Ecbatana. In the Bible there is the Book of Esther. She was a Jewish orphan. Through her uncle's intercession, she was married to the Persian emperor Xerxes, the biblical Ahasuerus. Esther dissimulated her faith and when the evil vizier condemned the Jews to death, she interceded and had them liberated. These events are recounted in the Bible, in the *Book of Esther*. Jews celebrate these events at Purim, shortly before Nowruz, the Persian new year that coincides with the spring equinox, 21 March.

The name Esther has many meanings. In Persian and Hebrew it means "star", but it also means "I will hide". Queen Esther dissimulates to save her own. And, in case of danger, we Shiites must also be able to dissimulate. Because, according to an ancient Persian proverb, "if at noon the King declares it is night, behold the stars".

Perhaps Esther was the one who taught my forebears to adapt truth to circumstance. Dissimulate so it will not be possible to publicly demonstrate your true nature, without risking yourself, your family, the community, the country. Dissimulating is still useful today. In the face of difficulties, of extremism, we react in one way by dissimulating and in another with the aesthetic of subversion. We can recite these verses by Hafez, one of our poets from the fourteenth century and a contemporary of Dante:

Let it, O heart, be that they'll open the wine-shops' doors,
Undo the knot of our business tangled up in failure.
Though they shot the bolt for the sake of the self-regarding ascetic's heart,
Be of good cheer: for the sake of God it will be opened.

They've closed the tavern door: O God, do not approve,
Because they'll be opening the door of deceit and subterfuge.

There is no generosity in anyone and the time of joy is fleeting.
The remedy is this, that we sell the prayer-mat for wine.
If you are intelligent and smart, don't let go of four things:
Keeping on the safe side, unalloyed wine, the beloved, and a private place.

Hafez also wrote:

Seek nothing extra. Take things easy:
A glass of ruby wine and a moon-like idol are enough for you.

Hafez, drink wine, play the rapscallion and be joyful, but
Do not, as others do, falsify the Koran.[3]

---

3   Trans. Peter Avery, *The Collected Lyrics of Hafiz of Shiraz* (Cambridge: Archetype, 2007).

The best wine? That of Shiraz, the city of the poet Hafez. Ruby red, with purplish highlights and an intense bouquet, in the seventeenth century it was also exported to the Catholic missions in Goa, in India. After all, as Omar Khayyam wrote, paradise begins on earth:

> Relinquish,
> relinquish everything
> in this world:
> fortune, power, honour.
> Step away
> from every path
> that does not lead you
> to the tavern.
> Ask for nothing,
> desire nothing,
> except wine, songs,
> music, love![4]

In the nineteenth century, James Justinian Morier said that when the Persians want to have fun, they get up early: they consider the early morning the best time to drink good wine, and they don't stop toasting until night. Today Shiraz – better known as Syrah – is a wine produced

---

4   Louis et Jean Orizet, *Les cent plus beaux textes sur le vin, Anthologie* (Paris: Le Cherche midi, 1984). Quoted by Jean-Robert Pitte, *Il vino e il divino* (Palermo: Sellerio Editore, 2012), p. 49.

around the world. It seems that Persia's medieval capital was known for making Shirazi wine, with one version resembling sherry. Syrah/Shiraz, a dark-skinned variety, seems to have been named for the Persian city, as according to legend the grape originated in Shiraz and was then brought to France by the crusaders. In any event, the variety is no longer grown in Iran.

* * *

In Tehran the art of subversion is not only the prerogative of adults. Grownups read Hafez and mothers teach this to their children from a very early age, reading them *The Little Black Fish*, a story by the schoolteacher Samad Berangi. The leading character is a rebellious little black fish. She abandons her mother and the brook where she was born to see what's beyond, to discover the sea. At the beginning a lizard warns her about the dangers involved, telling her about the pelican, the swordfish and the heron. The lizard gives the little black fish a thorn she can use as a dagger to cut the pelican's throat pouch in case she ends up inside it. There is no child in Tehran who has not heard this story and who does not consider that revolutionary little fish a hero, that little fish who, when betrayed by other fish and

35

facing death, says: "Death could come upon me very easily now. But as long as I'm able to live, I shouldn't go out to meet death. Of course, if someday I should be forced to face death – as I shall – it doesn't matter. What does matter is the influence that my life or death will have on the lives of others . . . ."

* * *

Persia is a timeless land and its name evokes an array of enchantments: mosques and minarets, architectural gems, lush gardens, majestic ruins rising in the solitude of the desert and vagabond tents, as described by Lord Curzon.

Persia's is a terrible beauty, and the Shiite saint Bahau'd-din Amuli said:

> If you look at it, every fresh blossom adorning this flower bed
> is a rose; if you pick it, it is a thorn.
> Contemplate the torch from a distance; do not draw near,
> for it looks like light, but it is all fire.

"Persia is a country in transition between past and present, a boiling mass of half East, half West. It is sharing these labels, but still has something that is more Eastern, in a very deep way, than

36

anything we know, and yet it's more Western than even we'd like it to be."[5]

Tehran is neither East nor West. It is the point of encounter between adjoining and independent civilizations, but it is always different. It is the emblem of the Iranians' *cultural schizophrenia*: poised between East and West.[6]

Tehran is a city with two souls, a city where you live straddling modernity and tradition. We are the citizens of a Republic – Islamic – and ours is supposed to be a democracy that is . . . religious, but in reality it is an oligarchy of ayatollahs and *pasdaran*. They are the pillars of a regime that was reinforced during the war against Iraq, unleashed by the army and air force of Saddam Hussein on 22 September 1980, following lengthy disputes about the southern border between the two countries. After the Khomeinist revolution, the Iraqi dictator feared that the ayatollahs might inspire a similar revolt among Iraqi Shiites, a majority that had been repressed for far too long. At the same time, he wanted to take advantage

---

5   Peter Brook, as quoted in A. C. H. Smith, *Orghast at Persepolis* (London: Eyre Methuen, 1972), p. 53.
6   Darioush Shayegan, *Cultural Schizophrenia. Islamic Societies Confronting the West* (Syracuse, NY: Syracuse University Press, 1997).

of Iran's seeming weakness. But the ayatollahs used the war as leverage to stir the nationalism of every Iranian and join forces against the enemy. Millions of young men left, wearing a plastic key around their necks to open the gates of paradise for martyrs. The conflict ended in 1988 following United Nations Security Council Resolution 598 of July 1987. The Iranians felt more and more isolated: Saddam used chemical weapons against them and not only did the West fail to lift a finger, but it also did not hesitate to sell weapons to both sides. To weaken them. This was the First Persian Gulf War, and it was one of the most violent conflicts following the Second World War. The ideology of the Islamic Republic was reinforced by this. A million soldiers killed in battle. Their widows? According to Islamic law, when the father dies the children go to his family. But the women refused to compound grief with grief, and they fought back. In the end, Ayatollah Khomeini gave them custody of their children. Like the women of Algeria during the civil war.

The Islamic Republic of Iran: a totalitarian regime in some ways, with a culture that is not standardized. Despite the difficulties, committed intellectuals and artists have been able to find channels to communicate. Their art is a weapon, a sword. This holds true for cinema: we can consider the director Jafar Panahi. After the disputed presidential elections of June 2009, he was arrested on 2 March 2010 along with his wife, daughter and about fifteen friends. They were at home, sitting around the table and talking about a possible documentary on the green movement. But the police burst in, accusing them of plotting against the state. Released on 24 May, on 20 December he was sentenced to six years in prison and was also banned from directing, writing and producing films, as well as travelling or giving interviews for twenty years. While awaiting the outcome of his appeal, in 2011 Panahi managed to film a documentary in the form of a diary, entitled *This is Not a Film*, which was then smuggled to Cannes on a flash drive hidden inside a cake. On 16 February 2013 his *Closed Curtain* won the Silver Bear for Best Script at the Berlin Film Festival.

Art is also a weapon for those who do satire: drawings often resemble realistic reportage, because the figures portrayed in cartoons are people we know – they are often around us. The images of caricaturists don't just laugh. They hate. Like the works of the German painter George Grosz between the two world wars.

* * *

In Tehran we blend East and West. We eat pizza, but our way, with *ghorme sabzi*, a typical local dish. And some people squirt ketchup on *zereshk polo*.

Would you like to visit Tehran? Don't expect to eat caviar! You'll find it at the airport – in the departures lounge – but certainly not at the shop down in the street. And don't expect to taste our typical dishes. Those are eaten at home. If you ask, perhaps someone will invite you. But don't listen to them unless the invitation is repeated three times: to be valid – and without bowing and scraping – the host must insist with his guest. Otherwise, you can't be served! It's a matter of manners, called *tarof*. It is faking brought to the nth degree. Iranians: fake and courteous, which is exactly what they say about the people of Turin.

But wait! It isn't always a woman in the kitchen. At our house, our father is the one who cooks. Our mouths watering, we say *dast-e shoma dard nakoneh*: "may your hands not hurt". Our father would say this to Grandma Mariam. And today, we say it to him. Dad cooks *fesenjoon*, made with duck breast from the Caspian Sea, chopped walnuts and pomegranate sauce. Or *baghali polo*, rice with fava beans and *shivid*, wild fennel, a long, thin green herb. My father always sets a handful of rice aside and tinges it yellow with saffron, Persian saffron extracted from the long, red and dense pistil.

And then we say *dast-e shoma dard nakoneh*, "may your hands not hurt", when my father cooks *abgusht*, a soup of meat and vegetables. It is seasoned with dried lemons sliced in half, which give it a wonderful tart flavour. In Persian we say *kheili khoshmaze*. The trick? Long cooking over a very low flame.

Another typical dish is roast lamb with pomegranate sauce, cooked slowly for hours. It is served with cardamom-scented rice. The rice is boiled and drained when firm, and then steamed until done, without overcooking it and making the grains fall apart.

Rose petals are my signature when, on the eve of Nowruz, I make a tray of baklava: with chopped pistachios, almonds, and two tablespoons of rosewater. To be enjoyed with black tea.

All of these are homemade dishes you'll rarely find in a restaurant. Away from home we want *kubideh*: ground meat marinated in onion and yogurt, wrapped around a spit that looks like a sword, and cooked over a flame by expert hands.

For the Iranians – even for those of us who have fled – food is a common denominator. It always unites us, regardless of which religion we profess and the many political ideologies that unfortunately divide us.

There's no McDonald's in Tehran, at least not so far. But we do eat sushi. Japanese cuisine is all the rage among Tehran's middle class.

We drink beer, but non-alcoholic, as spirits are banned. Or we drink *dugh*, yogurt thinned with water and seasoned with a pinch of salt and a few mint leaves. Do you find the idea disgusting? I understand, but I can assure you that it is very thirst-quenching. Starting in October you might also drink *ab-e anar*, pomegranate juice. A man with a cart sells it in the street. He drags the cart slowly, and to attract attention, every so often he shouts: *ab-e anar! ab-e anar!*

The pomegranate is one of the good things created by God and, according to the Quran, it grows in the garden of paradise. It is also highly considered in Judaism: it is one of the seven fruits listed in the Bible of those produced in the Promised Land, and the symbol of wealth and fertility, honesty and fairness.

In Tehran, at the end of a meal you'll have to settle for a cup of tea: don't expect an espresso. While in southern Italy it is obligatory to offer a guest a cup of coffee, in Iran coffee has a different meaning: it is drunk at funerals. *Qahve-ye shoma ro bokhoram* literally means that you want to drink your counterpart's coffee. But it is an idiomatic expression, meaning that you hate them and can't wait to attend their funeral!

* * *

In Tehran, women aren't always the ones in the kitchen and they do many different things. They study, work and play. Two summers ago, friends and I went to Laleh Park with water pistols. We played like children and were soaked by the end. It was hot. But some people weren't happy about it, so we had to stop. For us, games are serious business, even though religion and politics end up in the middle of things. Cards, chess, backgammon. The first cards to reach Iran were Indian and were sent by Babur, the emperor of India: 96 cards – sometimes 120 – in a deck. Made of cardboard, they were round or oval and were painted in bright colours.

Chess was called *shatranj* and is mentioned as early as the seventh century in an Avestic text written in ancient Persian, in *pahlavi*. In the *Book of Kings*, depicted in many Persian miniatures, Ferdusi narrates that chess was invented by the half-brothers Gav and Talhand, sons of the queen of India, who were in a battle in which Gav died. The queen ordered Talhand to explain how his half-brother died. He consulted the sages, who offered the queen an ebony board with a hundred squares on which two armies – one made of teak and the other of ivory – face each other, with a king in the middle. Next to him was the first minister (equivalent to the queen in the modern game), and on the sides two elephants holding a throne. Then came camels led by two wise men followed by two knights and, lastly, a fighter-*rukh*, where the *rukh* was a mythical bird derived from the proud Chinese phoenix, with flame-like feathers. It is a bird that can attack and kill much larger animals, such as the elephants and rhinos on which it feeds. These pieces move on the chessboard differently: the minister one square at a time, the elephants, camels and horses three squares at a time, and the *rukh* in any direction. They try to checkmate the adversary king and the army that prevents the other king from moving in any direction wins.[7]

We women of Tehran love to play backgammon, called *nard* in Persian. In the *Shahnameh* Ferdusi narrates that the Persian emperor Khosrow received chess from the Indian Rajah. A game, a challenge: the emperor of Persia and his sages

7   Norah M. Titley, *Sports and Pastimes. Scenes from Turkish Persian and Mughal Paintings* (London: The British Library, 1979), pp. 24, 26.

had to guess the rules. Unintentionally, the Indian messenger revealed that it was a war game, and after one day and one night, this clue allowed the minister of the Persian emperor to solve the mystery. In exchange for chess, the Persians sent backgammon to India: the Indians were unable to guess the game, and so they were forced to send Khosrow a double tribute.[8]

* * *

The women of Tehran have practised sports since the days of the shah. In 1958 Iranian sportswomen participated in the Asian Games in Tokyo. In 1966 the volleyball team won a bronze medal in the Asian Games in Bangkok. In the Asian Games held in Tehran in 1974, the fencing team won the gold medal, Mahvash won the silver and Giti the bronze. Under the shah, female athletes – in shorts or miniskirts – helped convey the image of a modern country. They were an element in the regime's propaganda.

And, in part, they still are, despite everything. Laleh Seddigh is a rally driver. In 2005, the thirty-five-year-old defeated the defending champion, a man. In July 2012 a director – born in Iran and

---

8   Titley 1979, pp. 26-28.

resident in the United States – made a film about her, with the approval and funding of President Ahmadinejad: his goal was to break down the negative stereotypes about Iran and its women, but his rivals and many filmmakers have not been of the same opinion.

So far, the women of Tehran have had little success at the Olympics. Recently, however, in Thailand the Iranian cricket team won against Kuwait. The women's volleyball team also did well in Indonesia. In December 2012, Najmeh won the gold medal in target shooting in China. And the following month in Vietnam, in the Asian tennis championship under 14, the young Sadaf Sadegh Vaziri played doubles with a Yemenite athlete, winning the final 6-0 6-1. Iranians smile when they talk about tennis, thinking about the champion Andre Agassi: he was born in Las Vegas to an Iranian father who is part of the Armenian minority. His real last name is Agassian.

Naturally, practising sports while observing the rules of the Islamic Republic is not easy. At the London Olympics in 2012 Arezou had to relinquish swimming and compete in kayaking. The seventeen-year-old had spent the previous six years swimming at Tehran pools during the hours reserved for women. However, Iranian law banned her from showing herself in public in a bathing suit. She didn't let this defeat her: wearing a light wetsuit and scarf, she got into a kayak and came in seventh at Eton.

On 11 July 2013 Elham Asghari won the Iranian record for women's 20-kilometre breaststroke in open-water swimming. Thirty-two years old, she swims in the Caspian Sea wearing a special costume that covers her from head to toe – and weighing 6 kg. But the Iranian Federation has refused to approve it. This wasn't the first time that Elham has been in conflict with the authorities of the Islamic Republic: in 2010 she decided to swim around Kish Island in the Persian Gulf. She planned to do it in three days, but after just 5 km a police boat collided with her, tearing her suit; the propeller wounded her legs. Her body gradually healed, but the psychological trauma remained. Elham wanted to quit but her father, a former Olympic wrestler, convinced her not to.

Many not-so-young women also practise sports. Katayoun teaches kickboxing at a gym in upper and middle-class Tehran. But she also gives lessons in the lower-class districts and even villages, where many women find kickboxing to be a way to let off steam.

We women of Tehran love sports. Skiing gives us a great sense of freedom. We go to Shemshak, located north-east of Tehran on the

Elburz Mountains. From the capital, it is an hour by car. These slopes for expert skiers were opened in 1958, during the reign of the shah. Or we go to Dizin: opened in 1969, it has pistes for all levels (including beginners) and a ski lift that reaches an altitude of 3,600 metres. The slopes are open from December to May. These resorts are crowded with *bacceh naneh*, spoilt young men on snowboards, while the girls are groomed as if they were going to a party rather than enjoying a sport. Unfortunately, as of a few years ago women can go skiing only if accompanied by their father, brother or husband: a male relative, a *mahram*. This is a way to strike women. Above all, however, it is a way to strike the middle class, which grasps every opportunity to challenge codes of conduct. Because people meet on the slopes, they set up encounters. And there are kilometres and kilometres of snowy pistes. The police can't always monitor us. Many women dare to ski without a scarf. This is why the religious police want to ban unaccompanied young women from the ski lifts. That's right, in the Islamic Republic we have the religious police.

* * *

We women of Tehran, love sports. We like riding bicycles, although we can only pedal through a few parks and not in our city streets, because it isn't easy to get on a bike while respecting the dress codes of the Islamic Republic. And very often we are blamed for the immorality of the society in which we live.

Like many other women, we too have caught "football fever". We have had a national federation of women's football since 1997. We play without a veil, but our fathers cannot enter the stadium to cheer us on. The first national tournament – with eight teams – began in February 2004. The athletes play on the country's most important fields. These are the same fields where the striker Khodadad Azizi and Ali Daei give their male adversaries a run for their money. They are the symbol of Iranian football. But when they play – the men – we women are not allowed to enter the stadium.

But every so often, we manage to get around these obstacles! In 1997 Iran's national team returned from Melbourne, where it had just qualified for the World Cup, and the following summer it played in France against the United States. Seventy thousand fans were waiting for the national team's return from Australia. Three thousand of them were women. We managed to get in and sat in a sector all for us. It had never happened before. In parliament a minority said they were in favour of letting women into stadiums on a regular basis. It was Tehran's spring and the president of the Islamic Republic was the reformer Mohammad Khatami. But he wasn't in command, as important decisions are made by the *Rahbar*, the supreme leader, who also decides foreign as well as nuclear policy.

Let me tell you something else about football, and the passion for it that so many Iranian women have developed. A few years ago, at Azadì Stadium in Tehran our national team played against Ireland in order to qualify for the 2002 World Cup of South Korea and Japan. The first match was played in Dublin and the Irish won 2-0. The return match was played on 15 November 2001 at Tehran's enormous Azadì Stadium. Three hundred fans arrived from Ireland. Irish fans, so foreigners: they had the right to watch the match as long as the women covered their hair with scarves and no one drank beer in the stands. We women of Tehran, felt we were discriminated against. Why were they allowed to enter the stadium but we couldn't? Not all Iranian women obeyed the ban imposed by the authorities. Some dressed like men, slipped into the stadium and watched the match. The director Panahi told this story in his film *Offside*. And the newspaper *Azad* wrote about it, as an aside to the results: Iran versus Ireland, and we won 1-0. But it wasn't enough to get us to the next round.

In the meantime, the conservative paper *Jomhuri-ye Eslami* published another article: "Many women would like to enter stadiums, but all this interest does not mean that it is ethically correct. We need merely think about how many people like to drink alcohol, use drugs and bet. That said, women watching the games at home, on television, is certainly appropriate: at the stadium, men swear and all this vulgarity is unbecoming for the other half of heaven."

The women's magazine *Zanan* rebutted this sarcastically, publishing two cartoons. In the first, a woman – veiled – on a terrace turns her telescope towards the faraway stadium. With one hand she waves a little flag and cheers. The second cartoon shows the road that leads to the stadium, lined with signs listing the items that are banned from the stadium: bottles, knives, clubs, chains... and women.

The managers also turned to satire. The date was 9 January 2003. At the Iran Khodro sports facilities in Tehran, Paykan was hosting Barq from Shiraz. The manager of the home team, Mahdi Dadras, got permission for a group of women to sit in a private sector. Because, after all, Paykan fans are extremely polite and don't swear! Plus, said the manager, "the presence of women in the stands improves the players' mood."

* * *

As you already know, Tehran is an anomalous city, a city of contradictions. Our economic system would like to be anti-American and anti-capitalistic. But Tehran has a stock market, just like Milan and New York. Called the Tehran Stock Exchange, it was established in 1967 and currently has 339 listed companies. Of these, 37 are automotive, petrochemical and mining industries. Most are public companies that were privatized over the past few decades. The logo of the Tehran Stock Exchange was inspired by an archaeological artefact made of metal, dating back to the Achaemenid period and discovered in Lorestan: four men hold each other by the hand, a sign of unity and collaboration. They are inside the circles of the globe that, according to an ancient myth, is supported by two cows, symbolizing intelligence and prosperity, similar to the way these animals are considered in India but vastly different from how they are viewed in Italy.

The contradictions of Tehran. Let's consider religion. In Tehran there are synagogues and churches, which open to the public, but there are no mosques for the Sunni. The mosques are only for the Shiites. If the Sunni want to pray, they go to the Saudi Arabian or Pakistani embassy. It is a matter of reciprocity: after all, over the years the Shiites were persecuted in Saudi Arabia and Pakistan, in Bahrain and the Emirates. The Shiites were massacred, tortured, raped, imprisoned, secluded, isolated like lepers. From the time of Ismail Shah, the year 1501, they have had a place of reference – Iran – where they are not systematically eliminated.

The contradictions of Tehran: homosexuals are condemned to death, whereas transgender people can change sex with the consent of a part of the Shiite clergy and receive compensation from the national health service (25%). Obviously, surgery does not solve their problems: in a conservative society, they remain on the sidelines.

The contradictions of Tehran. We women – and you foreigners as well – must wear a scarf to cover your hair. We women cannot take our little boys to the pool because mixing with men while wearing a bathing suit is a sin. Instead, the Armenians who live in Tehran have their own sports complex. But you're not allowed in if you're Muslim. In that complex, Christian boys and girls, men and women, can swim and experience the delightful sense of freedom we get from the lack of gravity. At that sports complex, Christians can play tennis on red clay, wearing capris. Without a veil. Without restrictions. There, Christian Iranians have more rights that we do, the Muslim women of Tehran. I'm not being argumentative. This is simply a fact: in the Arab-Sunni countries of the Gulf the Shiites are persecuted or not allowed the right to full citizenship, while in Tehran the Armenians, native Christians, have a huge sports complex all to themselves.

The women of Tehran? You have probably heard of the lawyer Shirin Ebadi, our Nobel Peace Laureate. You have likely read Marjane Satrapi's autobiographical graphic novel *Persepolis* and seen her films. And Azar Nafisi's *Reading Lolita in Tehran* gave you insight into our numerous difficulties. Your European dailies often talk about us. They wrote a great deal about Neda Agha-Soltan, killed in Tehran on 20 June 2009 during the manifestations of the green movement. They published articles on Sakineh, condemned to death by stoning for adultery, a sentence that was suspended thanks to Western pressure. But your newspapers don't always write that in Tehran the level of schooling is one of the highest

54

in Asia. School is free and mandatory until the age of fourteen. Boys and girls go to school and don't spend their days weaving carpets: child labour is against the law! And they don't spend their afternoons at the Quranic school. We get more than enough religion!

At the university, two out of three students are women. In 2006 the government set "blue" quotas to give men equal opportunities at the departments of medicine, dentistry and pharmacy. At the time, we laughed about it, but lately things have gotten worse. The authorities are trying to impose gender segregation at universities, which is something new for us, because when the University of Tehran was inaugurated in 1937, everyone could enrol – men and women alike – and sit next to each other. Iran's only women's university dates back to 1964 and was promoted by the last shah. Perhaps he wanted to imitate the United States, where there are women's colleges and they are prestigious. But not here: they are something new, senseless.

Moreover, since October 2012 women are not allowed to study mining engineering at the University of Tehran, while in Isfahan political science and business are restricted to men only. In turn, at Isfahan men can no longer enrol with the departments of history, linguistics, literature, sociology and philosophy. This is another senseless decision: we Iranians – men and women alike – prefer scientific studies. We want to become doctors, engineers, information technologists. Only 8% of us study humanities. Because with a degree in humanities you'll achieve little and earn even less. At most, you'll end up being a teacher.

* * *

The women of Tehran? They are many. And each one has left a mark on history, since antiquity. During the Achaemenid period Artemis accompanied the emperor Xerxes on the military campaign against the Greeks. Mandane, the wife of Cambyses, was the mother of Cyrus the Great: she established the first school in ancient Persia, and children also learn riding and archery.

In more recent times, we have Rostameh. A swordswoman with infallible aim, she was one of the leaders of the Zanjan revolt of 1850. Robabeh Marashi was one of the first teachers. Thirty years before the official opening of a girls' school in Tehran, in 1891 she taught girls in her home.

Anis od-Douleh was the favourite in Naser od-Din Shah's harem. Although she was not of noble descent, since she had contracted a temporary marriage and did not have children, she had great influence over her husband and thus the country. In 1873 she left for Europe with the shah, but the pressure of the Shiite clergy was so strong that when she reached Moscow she was forced to return. She defended the weak, criticized the shah's lavishness and in 1891 adhered to the ban on smoking water pipes, promoted by the religious leader Mirza Hassan Shirazi to protest against granting a tobacco concession to a foreigner. Her gesture was so persuasive that the sovereign revoked the concession.

Also during the Qajar period, Ashraf al-Saltana was the first female photographer, while Taj al-Saltana was the rebellious daughter of Naser od-Din Shah: she criticized the veil and uncovered her face. After being raised in the royal harem, she attacked the segregation of women, divorced and had a lifestyle considered licentious for her day. She promoted education, political activity and the participation of women in the world of labour. Even by the standards of her generation in Europe and the United States, she was a pioneering feminist. In her memoirs as a Qajar princess, through her own story – with a stern mother, a self-indulgent father, and an adolescent and bisexual husband – she illustrated the country's transformations. Taj al-Saltana set up a literary association and wrote that "today there is no more progressive ideal close to the freedom than socialism".

Education was the point of departure for women's emancipation, and not only for the women in the royal harem. In 1903 Touba Roshdiyeh founded a girls' school in a part of her home, calling it *Parvaresh* ("Instruction"). Four days after it was inaugurated, government employees threatened her and made her close the school.

Fast-forward to 6 April 1907. The newspaper *Habl ol-Matin*, published by Moayed ol-Eslam, wrote: "Five hundred women assembled in Baharestan Square shouting Long live the Constitution! Long live the law! Down with dictatorships and dictators!"

On 24 March 1907 the magazine of the parliament had an ad page for a girls' school. The first to found one was Bibi Khanum Estarabadi. The conservatives protested, going so far as to say that the education of women was akin to alcohol consumption and prostitution. On 10 May Bibi Khanum wrote an article in the newspaper *Tamadon*: "Bearing their own interests clearly in mind, some are frightened by the fact that women might understand something more and rebel against oppression, arriving at asking for rights that have been denied so far."

On 31 January 1908 a meeting of women was held in Tehran. They approved ten articles, including the foundation of girls' schools and other measures tied to women's rights. Kahal published the first women's magazine on 1 September 1910. Titled *Danesh* ("Knowledge"), it was a weekly and, in eight pages, it analysed women's issues, underscoring their social habits.

In the face of the tsar's ultimatum to the Iranian government and the Russians' threat to occupy Tehran, on 31 January 1911 the national association of Iranian women organized a demonstration in front of parliament. Thousands participated, boycotting Russian and English goods. In the early twentieth century, Bibi Mariam – known also as Lor-e Bakhtiari – was the leader of guerrillas for years, fighting against the English, who never managed to capture her.

On 2 July 1911 a group of Armenian Iranian women acted on the stage in Masudieh Park. And on 4 April 1911 member of parliament Vakil ol-Raaya raised the issue of women's right to vote, but all hell broke loose.

Diana Abkar was the first female diplomat of the twentieth century. Although she was Iranian, in

1919 she became ambassador of the independent state of Armenia in Tokyo.

Simin Daneshvar, the doyenne of Persian women's literature, was born in 1921. Her novel *Suvashun* (*Mourners of Siyâvash*, also known as *A Persian Requiem*), is about Zari, a young wife and mother who lives in Shiraz during the Second World War at the time of the Allied occupation. The leading character is tormented by the desire for a traditional family and that of her own identity. Daneshvar died in 2012. The four hundred women writers catalogued by the Ministry of Culture of the Islamic Republic – according to which there are more female than male writers in Iran today – owe a great deal to Daneshvar.

A native of Isfahan, Sedigheh Doulatabadi was born into a particularly strict family and was promised as a bride to an elderly man against her will, and she had to fight against her own family. Beaten for founding a school, of which she could not serve as the principal because of her family's decision, she wrote for a newspaper that was then banned. When he exiled her to Tehran, the head of the Isfahan police force commented, "She was born a hundred years too soon." She replied, "I was born a century too late. If I had been born earlier, I would not have allowed women to be chained to men this way." Starting in 1911 she was a member of the executive committee of the National Women's Association (*Anjoman-e Mokhaddarat-e Vatan*). She went to France to study psychology, and in the spring of 1922 she participated in the International Women's Conference in Berlin. This was the first time that Iranian women attended an international conference.

On 8 March 1921 Women's Day was celebrated in Iran in the northern town of Anzali. Truth be told, this was not the first time, because in ancient Iran Women's Day was commemorated on the 5th day of the month of Esfand, or 23 February. That day, *Sepandarmazgan*, is named for the guardian angel of the land and of good women. It is a day that men commemorated by bringing gifts to their mothers, wives and daughters. After the 1979 revolution, Women's Day was publicly celebrated for the first time on 8 March 2000 at the Shahr-e Ketab bookshop.

On 23 February 1928 Ali Vakili created the Cinema Zardoshtian for women only in the great hall of the Zoroastrian school in Tehran, in Naderì Avenue.

On 4 January the first official conference on women was held in Tehran. And on 19 January of the same year the first group of Iranian girls was sent to study in Europe.

Sedigheh Saminejad was a pioneer of Iranian cinema. She debuted as an actress in the winter of 1934 in the film *Dokhtar-e Lor*, playing the leading character Golnar.

On 8 January 1935 Reza Shah outlawed the veil. In March of that year the government allowed women to attend university.

In 1938 Ghodsi Afagh Adl Tabatabai was the first to graduate in pharmacy, followed the next year by Batul Homeyun Ehteshami with a degree in mathematics. In 1940 it was the turn of Mehrangiz Afzal and Zia Javid in natural science.

Fatemeh Sayyah, born in the Soviet Union to Iranian parents, was a well-educated woman with left-wing ideas. Invited back to Tehran to teach literature, in 1942 she became the first female professor. Secretary of the Iranian Women's Party (*Hezb-e Zanan-e Iran*), she oversaw the party journal demanding universal suffrage since 1944, calling opponents "medieval". Sayyah rejected the idea that a woman's main duties were towards her family, declaring that "there are no duties where there are no rights" and that "equality in marriage and divorce is the first thing Iranian women demand of parliament, the government and society".

Efat Tejaratchi was the first female pilot, making a solo flight on 20 October 1940. Monir Mehran was the first female reporter, specializing in sports. In June 1943, she and her husband founded the sports publication *Niru va Rasti* ("Energy and Honesty").

In April 1945 Nosrat Moshiri and other colleagues founded an association to promote children's education, also organizing classes for women.

Ashraf ol-Moluk Amini was the daughter of Mozafar od-Din Shah, a ruler from the Qajar dynasty. After the Second World War, she invested in a modern industry. They say that she tied a rope around her waist to enter the *qanat*, traditional aqueducts, to take a closer look at the work done by excavators.

In 1946, at the age of 26, the shah's twin sister Princess Ashraf was appointed to negotiate with Stalin for the return of several territories occupied by Soviet troops. She was received and when it was time to leave Stalin asked her to extend his warmest greetings to her brother, the Shah-in-Shah, and to tell him that if he had ten people like her, he had nothing to worry about. A strong and often criticized personality, she played a highly significant role. She described her meeting with

Stalin in her autobiography, *Faces in a Mirror: Memoirs from Exile*.

Raziyeh Shabani, arrested on 5 February 1947, was the first political prisoner in contemporary Iran. That same year Esmat Ghazi climbed Mount Tochal.

Yekatrina Saidkhanian, the first female lawyer, started practising this profession in 1949. In the spring of that year, Mehrangiz Manucherian, a graduate in jurisprudence and one of the first to enter the Senate in 1963, published a book criticizing the Constitution on the points where women's rights are denied. She asked for women's political rights, equal employment opportunities, court intervention in divorce cases, and the abolition of polygamy and *sigheh* (temporary marriages). In 1968 she received an award for human rights. In 1970 the senator criticized the law requiring women to obtain their husband's permission to travel outside the country. Six years later, the government announced that the husband's permission needs to be requested just once and is valid for a number of trips: a minor change compared to what was requested.

The magazine *Zanan-e Iran* ("Iranian Women"), the organ of the Hezb Zanan Iran party, was published for the first time on 20 May 1951. The permit had been granted to Safiyeh Firuz. Born in 1908, she participated in numerous international conferences. On 1 August the Society of Zoroastrian Women expressed its support for Prime Minister Mossadegh.

Shahla Riahi was the first female film director. On 9 September 1956 her film *Marjan* was shown to the public at the Diana and Khorshid'e no cinemas. In the meantime, the writer, jurist and poet Maryam Savoji dared to speak out for women's rights during a radio broadcast.

On 30 June 1958 the pianist Taniya Ashut won the first prize at the Paris Conservatory. Meanwhile, Setareh Farman Farmaian started a course for female social workers.

In 1961 Zafardokht Ardalan became Iran's first representative at the Committee for UN Women. Ten years earlier, she had founded the journal *Azadi-ye Zanan* ("Women's Emancipation"), serving as its director.

On 3 June 1961, the union of women lawyers made its voice heard, demanding universal suffrage, equal rights in all professions and other rights that had been denied until then. Female teachers and principals called for a one-day strike on 23 January 1963. For hours they handed out information about girls' schools and flyers asking women to stand up and support their right to vote, so that Iranian women wouldn't be treated like criminals. The Iranian oil company, banks and schools of higher education participated in the strike, which was held peacefully. Working behind the scenes were women's organizations. The following day, the daily *Ettelaat* published an article, saying "Yesterday secretaries, nurses, airline hostesses, receptionists, typists, teachers, doctors, telegraph operators and other government employees and office workers joined the strike to demonstrate the value of women in modern society. Their strike was held in most offices with the exception of hospitals and post offices, where it would have paralyzed essential services and was thus not held. At school, women teachers refused to hold class and instead gave conferences on women's rights."

Three days later, on 29 January 1963, women voted for the first time in the referendum to approve the *White Revolution* with which the shah of Persia launched a series of reforms to modernize the country. Voters in the referendum numbered 271,179 women and 5,598,711 men.

On 24 June 1965 the lawyer Ghodsieh Hejazi defended a man accused of theft and fraud.

Forugh Farrokhzad was the most famous Iranian poet, a troublesome figure for her era. Born in 1934, she studied painting and wrote verses in which she expressed her feelings as a woman honestly and openly, breaking with tradition:

My beloved,
with his bare bold body-
rose over his legs,
fearless like death.

On his firm face,
an array of fine lines-
was tailored by the revolt-
of his limbs.

My beloved surely belongs-
to a faded clan.

In the depths of his eyes, it seems-
A Tartar is constantly on guard-
for the advent of knights.

In brightness of his teeth, it seems-
a primal man- is patiently waiting-
for cornering a prey.

My beloved is like the earth-
in his blunt fated air,
in his concrete, cruel rule.

My beloved is wildly free.
My beloved is like a whole instinct-
In the core of a dark isolated isle.

My beloved is originally estranged,
like veiled gods, like lone monks.
My beloved is a male from the ancient eras,
and from the natural age of beauty.

By his tread, he awakens-
the innocent sense of youth.

With his aura, he reminds-
the fond flavour of mythical tales.

He loves with such a faith-
all bits of life, all tads of soil
all laughs and all the sorrows.

He loves with such a faith-
The void roads of the parish, the green veins of the trees
the slight smell of soap, the fresh taste of milk.

My beloved surely belongs-
to a faded clan.

My beloved,
He is a natural man.
And in this wicked wonderland
He must hide away.

My beloved,
He is a simple man.
And like the last rest of the vast past beliefs,
I hide him always away,
in the wake of warmth of my breasts.[9]

As a director, she has left us the short film *Khaneh siah ast* ("The House is Black") in which

---

9   Trans. Maryam Dilmaghani, September 2006, Montreal.

the leper hospital of Tabriz is the metaphor for a sick country. She died in a car accident on 13 February 1967.

A member of the Iranian Women's Organization – the president of which was Princess Ashraf while the vice-president was the mother of Farah Diba – Farrokhru Parsa became Minister of Education on 27 August 1968. Following the 1979 revolution, she would be accused of prostitution and executed; she was fifty-eight years old.

In 1969 Mehrangiz Dolatshahi became Iran's first woman ambassador and was sent to Denmark. Manijeh Farzad, Meimanat Chibak, Adineh Banimehr, Azarnush Malek, Shirin Ebadi and Homayundokht Homayuni were the first women to be appointed judges.

In the Seventies, Masumeh Seyohun was the first woman to open an art gallery in Tehran.

The first women's football match was held in the capital in January 1971. It ended 1-1 and the coach of the first female football team was Afsar Amininejad.

After the revolution, twenty-five candidates submitted their names for the 1980 elections. They were between twenty-four and sixty years old. Out of 270 members of parliament, three women were elected: Azam Taleghani (the ayatollah's daughter), Monireh Gorji (married, the mother of three married daughters; before the revolution she taught Quranic exegesis) and Goharolsharieh Dastgheib. In the Eighties other women entered parliament: Ategheh Rajai (widow of the assassinated president), Marziyeh Dabbagh (mother of seven and close to the great ayatollah Montazeri; she had been in prison and in exile in Syria and Lebanon) and Maryam Behruzi (married off at the age of just fifteen and the mother of four; before the revolution she held conferences and lessons on the Quran in the holy city of Qum, and under the shah she was imprisoned). They were from conservative families and tied to Islamic parties, and none of them ran as independents. Monireh Gorji was also the only woman to be part of the Assembly of Experts, a body composed of seventy members and dominated by the conservative clergy.

On 12 February 1993 Tehran hosted the Women's Islamic Games, an international event. On 16 July 1994 Iranian women participated in the Mathematics Olympiad for the first time. Zahra Sadr-Azam Nuri became mayor of Tehran on 19 November 1996. Nominated by the reformer president Mohammad Khatami on 23 August 1997, Masoumeh Ebtekar became Iran's first female vice president. Born in 1960, she became head of the Department of Environment.

Spokesperson for the Muslim Student Followers of the Imam's Line who on 4 November 1979 occupied the US embassy in Tehran, she is considered a reformist and her position was not renewed by the conservative president Mahmoud Ahmadinejad.

The Women's Police Academy was inaugurated on 14 June 1998. On 8 August of that year, Faezeh Hashemi, daughter of ex-president Hashemi Rafsanjani, founded the daily *Zan* ("Woman"). In the meantime, on 11 October, Jamileh Kadivar, Ashraf Geramizadegan, Parvaneh Mohii, Homeira Hosseini Yeganeh and Haleh Faramarzian created the first association of women journalists since the time of the 1979 revolution.

When you think about us, reflect on our courage, the strength of us women of Tehran. Because as a Persian proverb says, "Look in the sky to find the moon, not in the pond".

* * *

Women's rights? An ongoing battle. Some rights are denied, but not to everyone: members of the upper class have ways to get around these obstacles. Like the private swimming pools in the villas of Elaieh, a district north of Tehran.

We Iranian women have had the right to vote for fifty years, since 27 February 1963! Long before the Swiss, who got suffrage in 1971. In this legislature, nine out of 290 members of parliament are women. We got universal suffrage from the shah and Ayatollah Khomeini couldn't take it away from us. But the right to vote is not enough to make a democracy. The barometer of democracy is represented by women's rights, the rights of religious and ethnic minorities, the rights of those who have a different sexual orientation.

According to the law of the Islamic Republic of Iran, we are worth half compared to a man: when we inherit, when we testify in court, when we are the victims of violence. And, yes, there are femicides in Iran. According to the chief of police, 50% of the female murder victims are killed by a family member, someone living under the same roof. Polygamy is allowed but only under certain conditions, as the first wives are the ones who must give permission, but they rarely agree to compromise! At the same time, if we marry a foreigner we cannot pass Iranian citizenship on to our children.[10] This is a right that Italian women

---

10   On 2 October 2019 Iran's Guardian Council finally approved an amendment that would grant Iranian citizenship to the children of Iranian women married to foreign men. In May 2019 Iran's Parliament finally

obtained in 1983 and Moroccans in 2006, with the reform of family law.

For us, the women of Tehran, divorce is not easy and we do not always get awarded custody of our children. And this despite the fact that judges apply the "principle of competency", awarding custody to the parent best able to care for them, the one who will send them to school with their homework done and their clothes washed and pressed, and who will welcome them home to a hot meal. This is the merit of one of our many activists, like the lawyer Shirin Ebadi, our Nobel Peace Laureate.

As to rights, we should listen to our poet Hafez. *Sabr va zafar har do dustan-e qadimi hastand*:

---

adopted the proposed reform, but it went back and forth from the Guardian Council to determine whether it is in accordance with the Constitution and Islamic law. As explained by Human Rights Watch, "the issue has come to prominence in recent years because of tens of thousands of registered and unregistered marriages between Iranian women and Afghan men whose children are unable to obtain citizenship on an equal basis. Discrimination can harm children's access to education, healthcare, housing, and employment when they become adults. The latest attempt to reform the law was inspired by Maryam Mirzakhani, a world-renowned Iranian mathematician and Fields Medal recipient who passed away from cancer in 2017. Because her husband is not Iranian, her daughter cannot obtain Iranian nationality.

We must be patient, for patience is the companion of wisdom.

Much has changed over the past few decades. We need merely think that in 1977 Iranians had an average of six children, and women in rural areas eight. Today our fertility rates approach those of Europe: we don't reach an average of two children. It took three centuries for this to happen in Europe. Here, 74% of married women between the ages of 15 and 49 use family planning, 60% turn to contraceptives and the remainder rely on male or female sterilization.

Rights are an obstacle course. But I don't want to play the victim with you; I don't want to complain about the numerous difficulties also because, little by little, we are getting results. With a pinch of creativity, like my friend Leila. Her husband wasn't willing to grant her a divorce so she tried to buy it by relinquishing the *mehrieh*, the amount that the family and the mullah celebrating the marriage insert into every marriage contract. This means it has legal value.

It's called the *bride price*. It is a sum – money, gold coins or even a piece of property – that the groom must pay for the bride's virginity. It is a formality even for second marriages. It is effectively the price of divorce, as good parents would never give their daughter away without guaranteeing her proper protection in case of divorce in a social system in which women are almost always on the losing side from a legal standpoint. Particularly because a divorced woman without income is merely a *divorcée*, while if she is financially independent she is a *lady*.

Does he want you? He has to show himself to be generous; there is nothing worse than a skinflint. In any case, you – woman – are superior, and don't care about money. You don't demand immediate payment. You'll think about it only if, one day, he asks for a divorce. It is a way to dissuade him from leaving you… without adding things up. Because the *mehrieh* is indexed at the rate of inflation, according to the law of the Islamic Republic. Is he leaving you after twenty years? Then he owes you interest. Do you want to leave him? Then you tell him flat out, "I'll make your life impossible! You're better off letting me go!" The trade-off? You're a lady and you pay for your freedom. By relinquishing the bride price.

Then… are you afraid of being on your own? *Moshkel nist*, says my friend Leila: "Don't worry, *azizam*, the world out there is full of men ready to marry you!" To marry you for a while, a few months, a year. Then maybe you can renew the contract for a while longer. Are you tired of it before the deadline? Then you end the contract ahead of time. It's called *sigheh* and it is something utterly Shiite, utterly Persian, encouraged by the clergy. It's a fixed-time marriage designed as an outlet for one's sexual desires, because sexuality is not taboo for us. As long as it is consumed within the confines of some sort of marriage.

Sound strange? The fixed-time marriage is one of the many contradictions of the Islamic Republic. Today real marriage serves the purpose of procreation and *sigheh* to satisfy desire. Things used to be different: to avoid being repudiated, a sterile woman would allow her husband to take a temporary wife to bear his children. If the first wife was wealthy, she was the one who chose the woman who could sleep with her husband and procreate! Today, *sigheh* has its advantages: if you are a temporary wife, you each live in your own home and you don't have to wash his socks! And you're not required to tell your family. It can be a secret marriage. It has its appeal because, as the saying goes, *Zan bayad mesl-e mah bashe: shab biado, sobh bere*: The woman must be like the moon: she rises in the night and leaves in the morning.

* * *

Tehran is a woman. And like every Scheherazade, she whispers the right words. She is convincing. She enchants anyone in front of her. And she will enchant you too if you decide to travel there. Like a ruby mine, you will be open to the influence of the sunshine.

Our time here is about to end. I could tell you the adventures of the *Shahnameh*, Ferdusi's *Book of Kings*, the adventures set on Mount Damavand that my grandmother Mariam used to tell me. In Persian poetry, that peak is a white demon. According to legend, a three-headed dragon, the symbol of evil, was chained to those windblown slopes and condemned to remain there until the end of the world. For the Persians, Damavand is the symbol of resistance against foreign rule.

It is the highest peak in the Middle East. A cone of ice, a mountain that is a volcano, with sulphurous fumes that form asphyxiating fumaroles, and hot springs that cure every ache and pain. Its summit rises, snowy and solitary, north-east of Tehran. At dusk, kissed by the sun, it is a rosy ember in the darkening sky. The first woman to climb Mount Damavand, in August of 1940, was Teimuri, accompanied by several employees of the British Iranian Petroleum Company.

Grandma Mariam would tell me about Tehmineh, the daughter of the king of Sistan and

77

the wife of Rostam, the greatest hero of epic Iran, whose adventures are narrated in the *Shahnameh*. Sohrab was born from their love and grew up with his mother, because Rostam left the day after their wedding and never saw his son. Tehmineh is the symbol of the woman who – alone – raises her son, teaching him to love a father who is not there.

We women of Tehran, are also Tehmineh's heirs. And the heirs of the empress Seyyedeh Shirin Malekeh Khatoun, combative and wise, the regent in the place of her son, still too young to be king. She is buried and venerated at Shahr-e Rey, not far from the sanctuary of Bibi Shahr Banu.

* * *

And now let me tell you one last thing. As the mystic Rumi said, "The truth was a mirror in the hands of God. It fell and broke into pieces. Everybody took a piece of it, and they looked at it and thought they had the truth." If truth is a mirror broken into pieces, in these pages I have given you only one fragment. The fragment of my Tehran.

Azadeh Moaveni
AFTERWORD

Iran has been the central focus of Farian Sabahi's writing, her academic scholarship as well as her books and articles, for almost thirty years, certainly since I first met her in Tehran in 2006. Anyone who reads her work quickly realizes that Farian specializes in seeing all sides of Iran. Indeed she is most adept at identifying the country's many versions of itself, the sides it presents for the benefit of the gaze of the world, the sides it shows to itself, internally, and as well as its ferociously guarded and inevitably misunderstood interiors. That she has dedicated herself to peering into all these reflections, as intricate and shifting as the inlaid mirror work of a palace ceiling, is fortunate for her readers.

This particular piece, *We Women of Tehran*, is among her most artful and most subversive. She takes a form that Iranians have adapted cunningly to reveal their worldviews and agonies openly on stage, despite the limitations of the censor. Theater has flourished quietly in Iran for years, unexamined by the cultural eyes so preoccupied with cinema, until Asghar Farhadi's *The Salesman* revealed that it was actually theater, more than film, that was enabling Iranians to hold the most alive and ambivalent conversations with themselves about all the confusing and clashing realities of their society: the tragic way men also suffered their societal dominance, and the way even the most powerful and independent of women wished to be perceived as honorable in the eyes of men.

These questions of power and intrigue between the genders infuse the collective behaviors of the men and women of Tehran, and the way the capital has always been a staging ground for feminine agency and rebellion. Farian's text is visual: it sweeps us up and down the city, peering into the dilapidated, stubborn edges that the poor have inhabited for decades, as the great movement from the countryside to the capital began and never stopped, all the way to the tips of the mountains to the north, pausing to gaze at the boulevard that connects the two, all the while deliberating: why is this capital here in the first place, and why does it hide its charms? But more than anything, it portrays, through conversation and fragments of poetry and material observation, how the past pulses in the daily lives of the people of the capital. Tehran, where girls catapult over concrete walls in parkour flourishes, where they gather for flagellating mourning processions when the calendar their mothers have followed for generations summons them, where they frantically observe and judge the world outside, internalising its battles and trends into their own ongoing story.

Printed by
Digital Team – Fano (PU)
September 2021